ALAN SHEARER

HEROES

First published in 1997 by
Invincible Press
an imprint of HarperCollins*Publishers*
London

© The Foundry Creative Media Company Ltd 1997 (text)

A CIP catalogue record for this book is available from the British Library.

ISBN 0 00 218822 8

Created and produced by Flame Tree Publishing, a part of
The Foundry Creative Media Company Ltd,
The Long House, Antrobus Road,
Chiswick, London W4 5HY.

ALAN SHEARER

Introduction by Robert Jeffery

Main text by David Harding

ALAN SHEARER IS A FORWARD in the classic vein. Tall, dignified and supremely cool both off and on the pitch, the 27 year-old is the biggest name in British football right now, and the chances are he'll stay there for quite some time.

He signed for Newcastle on 30 July 1996, for a fee that was – at the time – the largest in the world. The fans waited for hours outside St James' Park to see their new hero; he took great delight in telling them: 'I'm just a sheet metal worker's son from Newcastle.' It was the start of a love affair that looks set to last well into the next century. For the fans, Shearer was the archetypal local boy come home. For Shearer, it was the ideal chance to impose himself on the World and European stages, as well as making the move back to his native North East.

Ironically, Alan Shearer could have signed for Newcastle much earlier than he did, and for a great deal less than his eventual £15 million transfer fee. As a youngster on Tyneside, his finishing skills were the envy of many a local club, and he had trials with Newcastle, amongst others. In the end, though, he had to make a journey of several hundred miles to find a club willing to take him on: that club was Southampton.

While at The Dell, he developed quickly from a gangly youth to a strong and determined centre forward. After a slow start, he went on to grab 23 goals over four seasons and to earn himself 11 England Under-21 caps in the process.

Kenny Dalglish and Blackburn Rovers were watching carefully. On starting at Ewood Park, Dalglish made the 22 year-old Shearer his first signing and his partnership with the more expensive Chris Sutton was to fire unfashionable Blackburn to the title in 1993. The fans worshipped Shearer and his career blossomed: he made his full England debut against France that same year.

Shearer's England career seemed, at first, like a non-entity: in 13 games, he did everything but score. The pundits were already writing him off. However, after scoring his first goal for his country there was no stopping him and by the time Euro 96 came around, Shearer was an established choice. His partnership with Teddy Sheringham was a winning ticket; their goals against Holland, in particular, alerted the world to the existence of the goal-grabber from England.

Despite the disappointment of failing to make the final, Shearer was big news by the time the tournament was over. Blackburn, bereft of Dalglish and struggling in the Premiership, could not refuse a £15 million offer from Newcastle owner Sir John Hall. Shearer was on his way home. He handled his first day at the new club with typical composure and modesty. Never one to boast to the press or hype himself, many commentators were moved to compare him to Nat Lofthouse or Stanley Matthews. He is, to be sure, a very old-fashioned player.

A record of 25 goals in 31 games in 1996-97 speaks for itself. A pre-season injury will rob Shearer of much of the new campaign – but France in 1998 is his target, and few would bet against his once again lighting up the biggest of stages.

Robert Jeffery

TYNESIDE CHILDHOOD

ALAN SHEARER IS ONE OF THE MOST famous footballers England has produced for years. Fast, brave, possessor of a fearsome right foot, strong in the air and a superbly consistent goalscorer, Shearer, for many, is the epitome of a typical English centre forward.

Aged just 27, Shearer has already tasted domestic and international success, has captained England, been transferred for a total of £18.3m and is set to be one of the most prominent footballers in the country for the next few years.

But despite his current riches – reportedly he is on £30,000 a week, a £1.8m-a-year contract and reckoned to be the 14th richest sportsman in Britain – the story of Alan Shearer begins in humble surroundings in Newcastle. The son of a sheet-metal worker, there was little to suggest Alan Shearer's life was to be different from the other boys he grew up with except for one thing – football. But this apparent ordinariness was later to be seen as an asset during his career by many in football who see Shearer's steady personality as a reason for his success, and a person who will only make the back pages of the newspapers rather than the front.

FOR A FOOTBALLER, Alan Shearer timed his entry into the world perfectly. He was born in August – the month that traditionally sees the beginning of the football season. He was born on 13 August 1970 in Newcastle, a time when the city's football club was experiencing something of a mini-boom in its fortunes. In 1969 Newcastle United had won the European Fairs Cup against Hungarian side Ujpest Dozsa 6-2 on aggregate.

As the young Alan Shearer grew up, the wearer of the Newcastle No. 9 shirt, now worn by Shearer himself, was Malcolm Macdonald, one of the biggest ever heroes on Tyneside. 'Supermac' as he was known, helped the club to the FA Cup Final in 1974 where they eventually lost to Liverpool. But his popularity as the rampaging centre-forward would not be matched until 20 years later – when Shearer donned the famous black-and-white stripes.

While at school, Alan Shearer played for Cramlington Juniors and captained the team at Gosforth Central Middle School, where the future England captain led his peers to a cup victory in 1982.

He was small for his age, not that quick and a bit one-footed.
Alan Shearer's PE teacher, Derek Rowland

OUTSIDE SCHOOL he played for Wallsend Boys' Club – who know a thing about talented youngsters. Their former players also include England internationals Peter Beardsley and Paul Gascoigne and Sunderland's Lee Clark. Like Shearer, Clark also went on to play for Newcastle at the most senior level. Indeed Shearer, Clark and Beardsley were all in the Newcastle squad for the 1996-97 season.

As he grew up, Shearer attracted the attention of several League clubs from all around the country. He played for Newcastle City Schoolboys and as well as bringing himself to the attention of the Magpies, he commanded interest from West Bromwich Albion, Manchester City and the team that eventually broke Alan Shearer into the big time, Southampton.

From the first time I saw him it was obvious he had what it took.
Jack Hixon, the scout who discovered Alan Shearer

AS A YOUNGSTER he played in almost every position including midfield and also proved himself a more than adequate goalkeeper:

I thought I could do everything. I thought very highly of myself. I thought I could score from corners, goalkicks. I was one of those kids that just wanted to do everything.
Alan Shearer

SHEARER was discovered by veteran scout Jack Hixon who recommended him to Southampton who had an extensive scouting and youth programme. On his trial for the Saints Alan scored five goals and the south coast club were, not too surprisingly, quick to offer the young star a contract. Other trainees at Southampton at the same time included England star Matthew Le Tissier, lifelong friend Neil Maddison from Darlington, and Leeds United's Rod Wallace.

PENSIONER JACK HIXON said when Shearer was later transferred to Newcastle that from the first time he saw the young star he knew he had the potential to become a professional footballer.

He was a coach's dream. He would listen, but, if he wasn't sure he wasn't afraid to come back and ask.
Dave Merrington, Alan Shearer's youth team coach at Southampton

ALAN SHEARER signed for Southampton as an Associate Schoolboy in 1984 and was taken on by the club as a YTS trainee the following year. Despite the attention of other clubs, including his beloved Newcastle, Shearer chose Southampton because he felt he would have more chance to develop as a footballer with the solid First Division outfit. Despite the current circumstances of the clubs, Southampton were at the time a more successful club than Newcastle and had been in the top flight since 1977. Newcastle were promoted to the then Division One in the same year – 1984 – as Shearer signed for the Saints, after spending the previous six years in Division Two. Their eventual promotion was secured largely due to the efforts of Shearer's idol Kevin Keegan, the man who, 12 years later, would smash the world record transfer fee to take Shearer back to his roots. Also in the Newcastle promotion team that year was Shearer's fellow Wallsend Boys' Club player, Peter Beardsley. Alan Shearer, though, was busy building his career at Southampton and was eventually to make his first team debut in 1988 aged just 17.

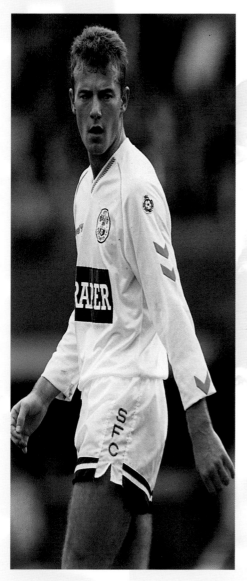

I just fancied Southampton - though I knew my dad would have loved me to have worn the black and white shirt.
Alan Shearer

He may have come down all the way from Newcastle but he was never homesick. This was no mummy's boy, this was a man's man.... The boy is a credit to himself, his family, the game, and everyone who's handled him during his career.
Dave Merrington

Ever since I first met him we have been very close friends. Alan has expressed the sentiment that I am like family to him and that means an awful lot to me.
Jack Hixon

SAINT SHEARER

Alan has the most important ingredient of all –
mental toughness. He can get bumps and
knocks and still play with them.
Dave Merrington

ALAN SHEARER ANNOUNCED his arrival on the football
scene in stylish fashion with a hat-trick on his first team
debut aged just 17 years and 240 days, the youngest ever
player to score a hat-trick in League Division One. This
broke Jimmy Greaves's record which had stood for 31 years.

Fulfilling his early promise and making sure that
right from the start of his career Shearer was a name
everybody would take notice of, the future England
captain scored three times in the first 49 minutes of his
debut – against an Arsenal side which included two
international defenders.

Saturday, 9 April 1988 may have been an ordinary
day for the rest of the football world, but for a teenage
Alan Shearer it was one of the biggest moments of his life
and the beginning of an illustrious football career.

Starting as he meant to go on, Shearer struck
three times for the Saints as they beat Arsenal 4-2 in a
Division One League match making him an instant
favourite with the crowd who gave him a standing
ovation when he left the pitch.

If ever Alan is needed by the first team I will
have no hesitation in recommending him.
Dave Merrington, before Alan Shearer had made his first team debut

ALTHOUGH it was the first time he had been seen on football's main stage he made sure it was certainly not the last time the world was going to hear of the talented teenager. It was a warning to the footballing world that a new star was on his way.

Six-footer with touch of midas.
Southampton Evening Echo headline 1988, just before Shearer's first team debut for Southampton

I would be surprised if any club could throw-up a better centre forward prospect. If they can, then the boy must be something special.
Dave Merrington, on a 17 year-old Alan Shearer

ALAN SHEARER'S amazing debut at Southampton came as little surprise to those who had worked with him including The Saints' youth team coach Dave Merrington. The man who would go on to manage the first team at the Dell said Alan Shearer had all the attributes needed to be a centre forward when the striker was only 17. An amazing display of faith in so new a player. His confidence was well rewarded – Shearer scored 48 goals for the youth team before he made his debut in 1988.

Every so often you get some players who will come on early and Alan just happens to be one of them.
Dave Merrington

SHEARER was to make his debut because of an injury to Saints' winger Danny Wallace who went on to play for Manchester United. In front of a crowd of 14,529 and wearing what was to become an unfamiliar No. 11 shirt, his fantasy start began after just five minutes with a header which beat Arsenal goalkeeper John Lukic. His second, after 33 minutes was a typically brave header. And he soon completed his extraordinary debut when he followed up one of his own shots to score his third.

SHEARER'S career at Southampton quickly alerted richer clubs to the fact that there was something special going on down at the Dell.

Week in, week out he gives 101 per cent and always conducts himself as a model pro.
Former Chelsea and Manchester United boss, Tommy Docherty

HE FORMED part of a talented trio of youngsters who were bursting through into The Saints' first team all at the same time, the others being Rodney Wallace who went on to win a League championship medal with Leeds United and the club's hero, England international Matthew Le Tissier. If Southampton had been able to hang on for all three, it could have been one of the most productive forward lines the country has ever seen.

You get some players who show tremendous ability during the week but can't produce the goods on a Saturday because of nervous tension. This boy doesn't suffer from nerves.
Dave Merrington

IN TOTAL Shearer scored 23 goals in 118 games for Southampton, the least productive time of his career, but his talent was firmly established. One of his most memorable evenings in the Southampton shirt was scoring a goal in a classic FA Cup encounter at Old Trafford when the lowly Saints dumped Manchester United out of the FA Cup in the early 1990s. It wasn't to be the last time that Shearer would haunt United with his goalscoring talents.

Alan is the complete centre forward.
Dave Merrington

ONE REASON why Shearer will always have fond memories of his time at Southampton is because that is where he met his future wife, Lainya, who was a secretary at the club. They married in 1991.

It's a grand day for Alan.
Southampton Sports Echo newspaper
headline, greeting Alan Shearer's debut
in 1988

*Stick him front of goal and
eight times out of ten, he'll
stick the ball away.*
Dave Merrington

*He told us he'd be a
millionaire by 25.*
Maureen Wareham, who Shearer lodged
with when he started at Southampton

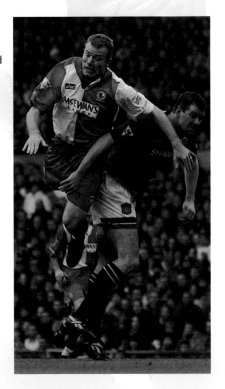

*He would get in any Premier
League side and score goals
for fun. Give him a chance
and he will score it.*
Teddy Sheringham

*Alan is a big, upright, old-
fashioned type centre
forward. He is a good
target man, a good contact
man. When you hit the ball
to him, it doesn't come off
him too easy.*
Dave Merrington

THE BLACKBURN YEARS

IN JULY 1992, ALAN SHEARER broke the British transfer record for the first, but not the last, time in his career. He was transferred from Southampton to Blackburn for £3.3m. The transfer put both Alan Shearer and Blackburn on the map: Shearer, because he was now playing for a team with serious designs on winning the League, and Blackburn because it proved they were a force to be taken seriously with the backing of chairman Jack Walker's millions and Kenny Dalglish as manager. This was also the first time that Shearer was supposed to have turned down Manchester

United, adding further to the kudos of Blackburn's record transfer capture. His deal was also financed with David Speedie moving to Southampton. By the time Shearer left Blackburn in 1996, he was an international football superstar and Rovers had won their first League championship for over 80 years and would appear in the European Cup for the first time.

In total, Shearer was to spend four years at Ewood Park, or to put it another way, 1,463 days. They were to turn out to be probably the most exciting four years even in Blackburn Rovers' long and proud history. The day after he signed, Rovers lost a friendly to Hibernian, but this wasn't going to deter Alan Shearer from making a big impression.

I would probably say he was the greatest player at the club, look at the things he achieved in just three years. If you mention Blackburn Rovers to anybody the answer you will get is Alan Shearer.
Paul Loftus

It was just the start that did us. Only Manchester United beat us in the second half of the season.
Alan Shearer

ON THE SEASON'S opening day he scored two superb goals against Crystal Palace at Selhurst Park as Blackburn won 3-2, and to prove his loyalty to his new club, Shearer theatrically kissed the club's badge on his shirt after scoring. He followed this up with the only goal of the game in his home debut against Arsenal. By December of that year he had scored 22 goals, before suffering the worst injury of his career so far – cruciate ligament damage – which was effectively to put Shearer out of the game until the following August.

You couldn't hope for anyone better than Alan Shearer to build a team around. He's the man I would want to take a last minute penalty for me or to hole the vital putt on the final green.
Ex-Leeds boss, Howard Wilkinson

HIS RETURN on 29 August 1993, was at – of all grounds – St James' Park, Newcastle. The game finished 1-1; naturally enough Shearer, who came on as substitute, scored the Blackburn goal. The next week saw him score against Sheffield Wednesday in his first full game since his return. The season 1993-94 saw Shearer score 31 goals which secured him the Football Writer's Association of the Year award as their Player of the Year.

The 31 goals was satisfying but I've never been motivated by anything personal. I'm motivated by the team and if the team's winning I'm happy.
Alan Shearer, on his 31 goals in his final season for Blackburn

Throughout the season, one minute we were up, the next we were down. We always knew it would be difficult and that it was very important to get a good start but unfortunately we didn't get that. Then the lack of confidence sets in.
Alan Shearer, on Blackburn's failure to defend their 1994-95 championship successfully

THE NEXT SEASON, in November 1994, Shearer scored a hat-trick against Queen's Park Rangers in a 4-0 win which took Blackburn to the top of the League. They would never lose that lead, and by spring were confirmed as the new League champions. Their success was largely due to the rampaging forward play of Alan Shearer. Throughout the campaign he scored 34 League goals and was the Professional Footballers' Association Player of the Year. Against Chelsea in December 1995, Shearer scored his 100th League goal.

As well as helping Rovers to the League title in his time with the Lancashire club, and scooping the individual awards, Shearer also became the fastest ever Rovers player to score 100 League goals. In his time at Ewood Park he scored an amazing 130 goals in all competitions in just 165 games – a phenomenal strike rate. In 138 League games, he scored 112 goals, a rate he has gone on to match at Newcastle.

That's us just about finished; totally buggered. Whether we like it or not Alan Shearer was Blackburn Rovers and now we have lost him we may have lost everything.
Blackburn Rovers fan, Stephen Dempsey, on Shearer's departure to Newcastle

HIS EVENTUAL TRANSFER to Tyneside was as much of a shock to the Blackburn fans as it was an unbridled delight for Newcastle supporters. While everyone knows that thousands turned up at St James' Park to greet the new king, hundreds turned up at Ewood Park unable to believe the news. One Blackburn fanzine compared it to the Kennedy assassination – everybody knew where they were when Shearer was transferred. There was also resentment among Blackburn fans that Shearer had signed for Newcastle having been in the first year of a four-year contract with Blackburn. But whatever the circumstances of his leaving, it is not too much of an exaggeration to say Shearer was probably the finest player to have ever pulled on Blackburn's famous blue-and-white quartered shirt.

You can liken it to what Cantona did to Manchester United. All the kids had blue and white shirts on with No. 9 on their backs.
Paul Loftus, editor of Blackburn fanzine *Loadsamoney*

He got the interest going again in football up here.
Paul Loftus

I thought he was happy here, but he wanted to go to his home club to play for the team he supported as a youngster.
Jack Walker, owner of Blackburn Rovers

WHEN SHEARER

left Blackburn, fanzine *Loadsamoney* said it was like the Kennedy assassination, 'only more important'.

Of course we'll miss Alan Shearer.
Lifelong Blackburn fan, John Pendle, on Shearer's transfer

EURO 96

THE YEAR 1996 CONFIRMED ALAN SHEARER as one of the most exciting and well-known talents in English, European and world football: he finished the season yet again as the top scorer in the English Premier League and he scored more than 30 goals in the season for the third consecutive year – a feat unequalled in modern English football.

Shearer also became the most expensive footballer in the world, captained England's national team for the first time and, because of his achievements in 1996, was voted the third best player in the world by FIFA, only finishing behind Barcelona's Ronaldo and Milan's George Weah.

And if all that wasn't enough, in the European Championships held in England, Shearer was the highest scoring player in the tournament with five goals scored in normal time.

The atmosphere has been unbelievable. I have never experienced anything like it.
Alan Shearer

EVEN BY his high standards, 1996 was an exceptional year for Alan Shearer. It ensured that he would be ranked as one of the country's most famous forwards following in a long and distinguished line of famous British players from the past and present such as Dixie Deans, Tommy Lawton, Jimmy Greaves, Geoff Hurst, Kevin Keegan and Gary Lineker. And it also made Alan Shearer one of the most famous faces on the world international football scene.

Shearer is now up there with Jürgen Klinsmann and Davor Sukar as the best in the business.
Former England striker, Trevor Francis

In Euro 96 we did everything as a team.
Alan Shearer

ALTHOUGH THE 1996 European Championships was an unqualified individual success for Alan Shearer, he entered the tournament under a cloud. Despite reconfirming his position as the best English striker in the Premier League by being its top scorer, doubts were being raised about his international future. At least one fellow professional had written in a national newspaper that he should be dropped because of his failure to score against a European international side for almost two years – a 1,065 minute scoring blank – as he entered the tournament.

Speculation had arisen that Alan Shearer wasn't up to the international grade. By the end of the tournament all speculation had been quashed and Shearer had established himself as the best striker in Europe and one of the best in the world with his magnificent displays during Euro 96.

I always had faith in my ability. Except for me not scoring goals, I always felt that I was doing reasonably well for England.
Alan Shearer, on his goal drought for England before Euro 96

Shearer's got a major, major reputation in Spain. They are all very frightened of him. For them he is a nightmare because he is the classic English striker, so complete, so fast, so powerful, good in the air and aggressive too.
Former Liverpool, QPR and Brighton striker, Michael Robinson, on the Shearer effect before England's Euro 96 quarter-final against Spain

ALAN SHEARER

IN TOTAL he scored in four different matches – once each against Switzerland, Scotland and Germany and twice against Holland. He also scored in the penalty shoot-outs against Spain in the quarter-finals and against Germany in the semi-finals. He ended up as top scorer for the whole tournament with a total of five goals. One of the most familiar sights of the tournament was to become Alan Shearer wheeling away in triumph with his right arm raised high saluting yet another goal. Not bad for someone whose England future was being questioned before the tournament. There's also no doubt his performances for England added a further £4m or so to his transfer fee which the world was soon to find out.

If you do not win private battles with a player you are in trouble as a team. We lost ours and Shearer took advantage.
Dutch coach, Gus Hiddink, after the 4-1 thrashing by England

Shearer Clogs 'Em.
The Sun's headline after the victory over Holland

HIS TALENTS not only won him the respect of the English fans but also fellow players and coaches from this country and throughout Europe, with famous stars such as former German defender and coach Franz Beckenbauer being one of those who praised England's No. 9.

He has confirmed himself as England's greatest striker.
The Sun

HIS GOAL against Switzerland, in the opening game of the tournament, dispelled any doubts that Alan Shearer should have been dropped. A header against Scotland, where he came up against his friend and fellow Blackburn team-mate, Scotland's Colin Hendry, added to his tally. Two goals in England's finest international performance for years, the 4-1 thrashing of Holland, confirmed that he was the man to lead England's attack. The Spanish side in the quarter-finals knew how dangerous he was and he was marked closely and failed to score. He did, however, score one of the penalties in the shoot-out at the end of the game. An early header against the eventual winners, Germany, proved Shearer could score at the very highest level. Shearer's flawless displays resulted in only one regret – England failing to win the title after they were knocked-out in the semi-finals.

45

The hitman of the tournament.
The Sun

It was a matter of days. I didn't have a choice about when I had the operation. The injury wouldn't let me carry on. It was a case of either having it done then or not playing in Euro 96.
Alan Shearer, on the groin injury that nearly kept him out of the Euro 96 tournament

As for Alan, he is the striker of the tournament so far. He has shown when it comes to the competition he is there and he's our man. He's a great all-round player and that is why he is No. 1.
Teddy Sheringham

We've put a smile on everyone's faces.
Alan Shearer, on the effect England's performances had on the nation during Euro 96

COMING HOME

ON 29 JULY 1996, ALAN SHEARER made headlines all over the world when he became the most expensive footballer of all time. Newcastle United paid a world record £15m for the England striker, sending Tyneside into delirium.

The fee confirmed Shearer as one of the most sought-after and exciting footballers in the world and beat the existing record set by Barcelona only the previous month when the Catalan club paid £13.25m to the Dutch club PSV Eindhoven for the Brazilian prodigy.

Although the fee has since been broken by Ronaldo's transfer to Inter Milan, Shearer's fee still makes him the most expensive British player of all time by over £6m. Previously, the highest transfer fee was the £8.5m spent by Liverpool on Stan Collymore in 1995, which was smashed by Shearer.

Ironically, Newcastle could have saved themselves £15m by signing Shearer when he was a schoolboy but he chose to start at Southampton.

But the money was an irrelevancy to Newcastle's fanatical 'Toon Army' who saw the capture of Shearer as the final piece of the Championship jigsaw and the return home of the city's prodigal son.

I decided to return home.
Alan Shearer, on why he signed for Newcastle

I am ecstatic like everyone at the club. We've signed the best for the best. It's lovely to see a Geordie coming home.
Kevin Keegan

SHEARER'S transfer to Newcastle caused an outbreak of excitement in the city that has rarely been matched in British football. Thousands of fans flooded to St James' Park, the home ground of Newcastle United, when news spread that England's most famous striker had signed for his home-town club in a world record deal. About 10,000 fans were estimated to have gone to the ground on the day of the transfer.

It's like dying and going to heaven.
Newcastle fan, Stephen Lockey, after hearing Newcastle had signed Alan Shearer

EVEN FOR A CITY that is probably more passionate about its football than any other in England, the scenes of delight were unparalleled. They were more suited to Italian or Spanish football when thousands turn up to greet a new, expensively-signed hero.

His transfer caused a rush in merchandise and season-ticket sales. Immediately after his transfer £70,000 worth of replica Newcastle United shirts were sold by the club shop. And in less than 24 hours an extra 100 season tickets were sold by Newcastle.

We have had a woman on the air crying and another, a mechanic, has downed tools to visit the club ticket office to try and get a refund on his season ticket.
BBC Radio Lancashire spokesman, on Blackburn fans' reaction to the sale of Alan Shearer to Newcastle

THE NEWS that home-town boy Alan Shearer had been captured was made even more special by the fact that he had been signed despite the attentions of arch-rivals Manchester United. His decision to go to Newcastle was the second time he had apparently snubbed United's boss Alex Ferguson, who had originally tried to sign Shearer when he opted for Blackburn. Many fans thought his presence was to prove decisive in Newcastle's chase to win the Premier League, the first time the team would have won the top League prize since 1927. They were eventually to finish as runners-up again – to Manchester United.

Despite the enormity of the fee – almost five times the amount Blackburn had paid for Alan Shearer – many in football realised that Newcastle had signed themselves the best English striker presently playing.

People query the fee, I say forget it. If you want to be the best you get the best, even if it means £15m.
Dave Merrington

We are the biggest thinking team in Europe now.
Kevin Keegan, after signing Alan Shearer

FOR SHEARER the transfer was a dream come true. He was born in Newcastle, and as a boy he had supported the team and had regularly gone to watch their games. Rumour has it he was one of the club's ball boys when Kevin Keegan played his final game for them against Brighton. He had a chance to sign for the Magpies when he was younger but felt he would become a better player if he went elsewhere first, away from the spotlight.

I wanted to play for Newcastle. Kevin Keegan was a big influence. On one hand, I'd always wanted to play for the club and he didn't really have to sell it to me. I knew what it was all about. But on the other hand I was talking to one of my heroes, a man I had paid to watch as a kid.
Alan Shearer, on why he wanted to come home

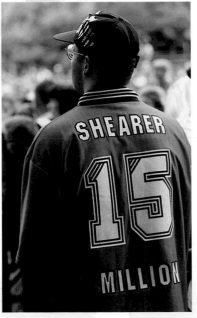

DESPITE the circuitous route, he had eventually joined the club he had loved all his life, and he was signed by one of his biggest ever footballing heroes – Kevin Keegan. As a youngster Shearer used to watch Keegan from the terraces of St James' Park. Now he was returning to the club when Keegan was manager. He described Keegan as 'his idol' and as a youngster had entered and won a local newspaper competition where the prize was to spend a day with Kevin Keegan. He was even photographed with Keegan, a photo that was, years later, to be shown all over the world. The feeling of admiration was mutual. Keegan described Shearer as his 'favourite player'. But despite his love of Newcastle, it had never stopped Alan Shearer playing well against his home team when he played for others. Just months before, he and another Geordie, Graham Fenton, had put paid to Newcastle's 1996 championship hopes with their performances in a 2-1 victory over Newcastle for Blackburn at Ewood Park in a crucial end-of-season clash. Shearer later said that he 'was just doing his job'.

Yes we've got the big one we wanted. This is a signing for the people of Newcastle.
Kevin Keegan, former Newcastle manager, after signing Alan Shearer

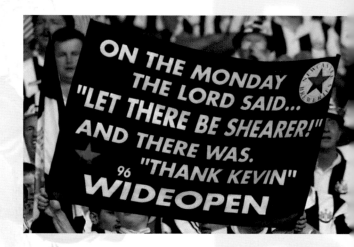

All I ever wanted to do was play for Newcastle. I'd stand on the terraces dreaming of the day I would walk out on the hallowed turf.
Alan Shearer

I just love signing big players and there is none bigger than this one.
Kevin Keegan

The match made in heaven.
Sun journalist, Martin Samuel, about Shearer teaming up with fellow-England striker Les Ferdinand at Newcastle

SHEARER AT NEWCASTLE

ALAN SHEARER'S TRANSFER to Newcastle instantly made many pundits believe that 1997 was the year the Toon Army would finally win the League again, and end a 70-year championship drought for the Tyneside club. In many people's eyes Shearer's transfer made Newcastle the favourites to win the championship: his forward play would be the final piece in the title challenge jigsaw. Newcastle had only narrowly failed to lift the title the previous season. Despite leading the championship race for many months and winning fans over with their attacking style of play, heartbreak was in store for the Newcastle fans as their team faltered, losing memorable games at Liverpool and Blackburn and at home to Manchester United. They were eventually pipped at the championship post by Manchester United and had to settle for the position of runners-up. For all their disappointment this was still their best position for years.

But Shearer's transfer was, for many, the turning point in Newcastle's quest to land the championship. He would team up with his England striking partner Les Ferdinand to terrorise Premiership defences, and with other stars such as Beardsley, Ginola, Asprilla and Batty, expectations were high on Tyneside that 1997 was going to be Newcastle's year.

*My confidence never changes. I go into
every game thinking I can score.*
Alan Shearer

*He's a great player. I would have
preferred it if he hadn't been playing.*
**Leicester manager, Martin O' Neill, after Shearer's 13-
minute hat-trick had destroyed his team**

BUT NEWCASTLE'S 1996-97
Premiership assault was to turn out
rather differently than everyone
expected: their season started with a
humiliating 4-0 defeat at Wembley by
old adversaries Manchester United;
they were knocked out of the FA Cup
by Nottingham Forest, who would
eventually be relegated to the First
Division; and were sent crashing out of
the Coca Cola Cup by north-east rivals
Middlesbrough. But that was nothing
compared to the shock news on 8
January 1997, when Tyneside god Kevin
Keegan sensationally quit as manager
after five years in charge. The man
Shearer revered as an idol – and one of
the main reasons why he had joined
Newcastle – amazed the football world
with his departure.

If I was asked about my legacy at St James' Park, probably my proudest achievement was that I brought Alan Shearer home. For years we had local talent leave. Now for the first time we brought some back. And not just any player either. I think we got the greatest of all.
Kevin Keegan

JUST A WEEK later Newcastle appointed Alan Shearer's old boss from Blackburn, Kenny Dalglish, as the new manager on a three-and-a-half year contract. For Dalglish it was history repeating itself: he had replaced Keegan as the new messiah at Liverpool as a player 20 years earlier. For Shearer, Dalglish was possibly the only man who could have replaced King Kevin.

I'm lost for words when it comes to describing Shearer's achievements.
Present Newcastle boss, Kenny Dalglish

DESPITE all the changes on Tyneside one thing remained very familiar – Alan Shearer scoring goals – and lots of them. Wearing his favourite No. 9 shirt, which he had requested when he signed for Newcastle in the summer, Shearer, in just 31 League games during the 1996-97 season, scored an incredible 25 goals – almost a goal a game – and he also bagged one each in the FA and Coca-Cola Cups despite the poor cup runs.

I think it is a very long time since this country produced a footballer so revered on and off the field, by everyone from fans to fellow professionals.
Kevin Keegan

The England skipper's match-winning brilliance has left a long trail of despairing defenders in its wake over the years.
John Edwards, *Daily Mirror* journalist

HIS TOTAL made him the FA Carling Premiership's leading marksman for the season, two ahead of his nearest rival, Arsenal's Ian Wright, and confirmed that even at £15m Shearer did not look overpriced. He scored his first goal for the club on his home debut against Wimbledon in front of a delirious and packed St James' Park. In case anyone thought that was a flash in the pan, he followed that up with the only goal of the game in the next match against Sheffield Wednesday.

Al Capone.
***The Sun* newspaper headline describing Shearer's goalscoring powers**

BETWEEN 14 SEPTEMBER

1996 and 20 October 1996 he scored five goals in consecutive games including the third goal in Newcastle's best win of the season, the 5-0 home demolition of champions Manchester United.

Shearer was rampant throughout the season. Just after Christmas he scored nine goals in seven games. Three times he scored twice, against Tottenham, Leeds and Chelsea, and an incredible hat-trick in just 13 minutes against Leicester City as his goals completed an incredible comeback turning a 3-1 defeat into a 4-3 victory. He was the club's penalty-taker for the season which added three further goals to his tally.

Alan Shearer staged an astonishing one-man rescue act that had thousands of Newcastle fans punching the air.

Daily Mirror journalist, John Edwards, on Shearer's hat-trick against Leicester

FOR A WHILE he looked as though he was going to make mugs of the bookies who offered prices of 500-1 against any player scoring against every Premiership club in one season. In the end he only failed to score against three clubs, Middlesbrough, Southampton and West Ham United, and this was partly due to injury.

But Shearer's season was rounded off in style when he again received the accolade of his fellow professionals who named him the Professional Footballers' Association Player of the Year for 1997, the second time he had won that award.

That was the most painful defeat of my career.
Martin O'Neill

Storybook Shearer hits a 13-minute hat-trick.
Guardian newspaper headline, greeting Shearer's exploits against Leicester

ENGLAND CAPTAIN

ON 1 SEPTEMBER 1996, ALAN SHEARER reached the pinnacle of his career so far, when he captained England for the first time. In a World Cup qualifier against Moldova in Chisnau, Shearer led out an England team for the first time which included Paul Gascoigne, Paul Ince and David Beckham. England won 3-0 and naturally enough Alan Shearer scored. He was later to describe it as one of the proudest moments of his life. If ever anyone seemed destined to captain England, it was Alan Shearer, right from the moment he started out on his football career at Southampton.

The game was Shearer's 29th for England and his international career stretches back to 19 February 1992 when he made his debut at Wembley against France. At the time he was still playing for Southampton. He announced his arrival on the international football scene with a goal on his debut against a French side that included former Manchester United star Eric Cantona. England won 2-0. Just as his first England goal was scored against France, so was his most recent. Before Alan Shearer's current injury problems, he scored the only goal of the game, a last minute strike in Montpelier in a 1-0 victory during the Tournoi de France in the summer of 1997.

If you can't take the pressure you should not be in football.
Alan Shearer

There's no doubt about it, he's one of the most magnificent strikers in the world.
Terry Venables

I regard Alan Shearer as the finest striker in the world.
Professional Footballers' Association chief, Gordon Taylor

IN TOTAL he has played 35 times for England, scoring 16 goals. Three of those performances came while he played for Southampton; 25 when he played for Blackburn; and seven so far in his time at Newcastle. His England career now spans five years and three different managers. He was given his chance under Graham Taylor, then selected by Terry Venables and was given the captain's armband by the current England coach, Glenn Hoddle.

Becoming England captain is one of the greatest things that has happened to me in football. There's not many things that can beat skippering your country. It's a great honour for me.
Alan Shearer

The public image is not the real Alan. He is the most impressive character I have worked with and if I had to put my faith in one individual, my choice would be Shearer.
Kevin Keegan

SHEARER was also selected for England's disastrous European Championship campaign in Sweden in 1992, but he made only one appearance in the tournament, against France, in a dull 0-0 draw. At the time he was competing for a place in the England team against the second-highest English goalscorer of all time, Gary Lineker.

He's probably the best centre-forward in Europe. He shows great anticipation, works on and off the ball and is a natural goalscorer.
Arsenal and Holland's Dennis Bergkamp

FOR ALL THREE managers Shearer was to become a mainstay of the team and the only problem has usually been who to choose as his striking partner.

I knew he would never let me down.
Kevin Keegan

SINCE EURO 96 Shearer has teamed up most effectively with Manchester United's Teddy Sheringham. The value and understanding of their partnership has been demonstrated in many matches. In May 1997, they scored a goal each in the crucial tie against Poland in Katowice which England won 2-0. The previous game they had again scored both goals between them in another 2-0 victory, this time against Georgia.

One Chance......One Shearer.
The Sun newspaper headline, before England's World Cup clash with Italy

DURING ENGLAND'S present World Cup campaign Alan Shearer has scored five times in just five games. He scored both goals in England's stuttering performance against Poland in October 1996, his second match as captain. The only game in which he has failed to score was the home defeat by Italy. Injury ruled him out of the game in Georgia which England won 2-0. The two goals were scored by the men who have partnered Shearer most during his England career, Teddy Sheringham and his former Newcastle team-mate Les Ferdinand.

*The man's the best.
It's as simple as that.*
**Former Liverpool and Eire
defender Mark Lawrenson**

*Alan Shearer can score goals,
no doubt about that. He's a
typical striker, a typical finisher.*
Germany's Jürgen Klinsmann

ALTHOUGH HE has yet to score a hat-trick for England, he has scored two goals on three separate occasions. The two against Poland in the World Cup, against Holland in Euro 96 and against the USA in a friendly in September 1994, England won 2-0. Despite his well-documented barren spell before the Euro 96 championships, Shearer, prior to his injury at the beginning of the 1997-98 season, has now struck his richest vein of form as an international. The England goalscoring record is held by Bobby Charlton, who hit the net 48 times for his country. As Shearer's striking record continues to improve for England, this long-standing record could come under threat.

Like Kenny Dalglish, Alan will never let his guard down in public. Why should he? But like Kenny he can be funny, good company and a world apart from the way others perceive him. It is Alan's hidden qualities which set him apart from the rest.
Kevin Keegan

Playing in the World Cup is any player's ambition
Alan Shearer

Behind closed doors, Alan is one of the most brutally honest people I know.
Kevin Keegan

Whatever happens in life no-one can take that away. It happened to me, to be England captain, and that hasn't happened to too many footballers. Money can't buy that, can it? Being England captain; you can't put a price on that.
Alan Shearer

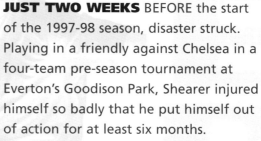

MISSION POSSIBLE

JUST TWO WEEKS BEFORE the start of the 1997-98 season, disaster struck. Playing in a friendly against Chelsea in a four-team pre-season tournament at Everton's Goodison Park, Shearer injured himself so badly that he put himself out of action for at least six months.

Stretching for a pass in the last minute of the game, Shearer fractured a fibula, ruptured ligaments on both sides of the ankle, chipped a bone and displaced a joint.

The injury was not only a massive personal blow to Shearer, but also to Newcastle's championship challenge and England's hopes of qualifying for the World Cup finals in France in 1998. Instead of leading the charge for both club and country, Shearer was instead having to battle against serious injury. The injury happened just days after Newcastle had agreed to sell striking partner Les Ferdinand to Tottenham leaving Newcastle apparently light up front.

He's overcome injuries before. He knows how to cope. We will give him all the encouragement we can. The good news is that he is a fast recoverer.
Glenn Hoddle

It's like opening a box of chocolates on Christmas Day and finding that your favourite one is missing.
Newcastle fan, Chris Green, on the news of Alan Shearer's pre-season injury

He's got the all-round game, he's got everything.
Mark Jenson

BUT ONE THING both Kenny Dalglish and Glenn Hoddle can be sure of is that Alan Shearer will be back. He has faced serious injury problems before and overcome them. In 1992 he damaged cruciate ligaments when playing for Blackburn, and during the 1996-97 season, due to a groin injury, he missed several crucial games for Newcastle. He ended up playing only 31 games out of a possible total 38 League games and five cup games, but he still ended as the season's top scorer in the Premier-ship. Shearer's ambition and will-power mean that he will get himself fit again as soon as possible. Shearer himself has already said he will be back this season to lead Newcastle and England, and England coach Glenn Hoddle is confident he will be back playing in the England shirt.

I know I will be back, but it's a matter of when.
Alan Shearer, on his injury

It's one of those things, people might think Shearer coming home makes a good story, but Shearer was a fan in the early days when Keegan was playing.

Newcastle fan, Mark Jenson, editor of Newcastle United's *The Mag* fanzine

SHEARER'S main aim when he does return is to get himself fit for the summer World Cup. Even though he will miss the crucial World Cup qualifier in Rome in November, a fit Shearer would be a certainty to play for England, if they qualify for the World Cup in France.

After the World Cup he has a chance to complete his second full season for Newcastle. But if he performs well in France, there is no doubt he would be chased once again by the top clubs in Europe.

In a few years' time he might like to have the experience of playing on the continent because he has always been so ambitious.

Mark Jenson

81

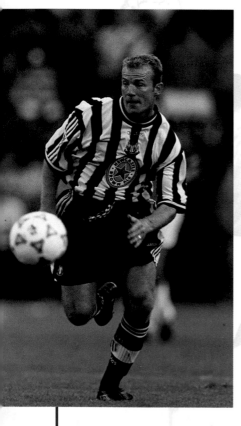

ALTHOUGH he currently plays for his beloved Newcastle, a move abroad eventually could not be ruled out and there would be many clubs queuing for the signature of one of the best strikers in the world.

Juventus were after me but I wanted to play for my home town club. I have a contract for five years and although I would be willing to play in Italy, it would be a big surprise if Newcastle were to sell me.
Alan Shearer

SHEARER himself has not denied the possibility of going abroad at some stage in his career, though only a very few clubs in Italy or Spain could probably afford to buy him.

Newcastle means more to him than just any other club.
Mark Jenson

WHATEVER HAPPENS, Shearer is bound to remain one of the major stars of English football for the next few years. Quiet off the pitch, Shearer's ambitious and determined streak on the field will ensure that he will terrorise more defences in the future whether he is playing for Newcastle, England or even for another team. By the end of the World Cup next year there is every chance that instead of being rated the third best forward in the world, Alan Shearer could be number one all over the planet.

It is part and parcel of the game.
Alan Shearer, on injuries

Alan will be back, you can be sure of that. Obviously it is a blow for Newcastle and for England, but I have spoken to him and, as expected, he was very positive.
England coach, Glenn Hoddle, on Shearer's latest injury

If you compare him to the last two managers he does take after Dalglish rather than Keegan. He has a dry sense of humour like Dalglish.
Mark Jenson

I know that I'm going to have ups and downs over the next couple of months but I've been in this position before. I suppose I am lucky in one sense in that I know what's going to be coming along.
Alan Shearer

FACT FILE

- *Full Name:*
  Alan Shearer
- *Height:*
  6'0"
- *Weight:*
  11st 2lb – 12st 1lb
- *Born :*
  13 August 1970 in Newcastle,
  England.
- *Career:*
  As a junior, represented
  England at B-team level,
  Under-21 & Youth levels.

Southampton as Associate
Schoolboy from 1984, later signed as YTS Trainee and eventually
signed from Trainee on 14 August 1988: FL 105 appearances (13 subs,
23 goals); FLC 16 appearances (2 subs, 11 goals); FAC 11 appearances
(3 subs, 4 goals); Others (8 subs, 5 goals).
Blackburn Rovers from 24 July 1992 for £3.3 million: PL 132
appearances (6 subs, 112 goals); FLC (16 subs, 14 goals); FAC (8 subs,
2 goals); Others (9 subs, 2 goals).
Newcastle United from 29 July 1996 for £15 million.
England Team from 12 December 1995.

SHEARER'S GOLDEN MOMENTS

- *July 1992*
  In the opening game of the season, Shearer scores two goals
  against Crystal Palace at Selhurst Park, helping Blackburn to
  their 3-2 victory.
- *29 August 1993*
  Shearer's return to the game, after recovering from extensive and
  excruciating ligament damage, is marked by his goal in the 1-1
  draw against Newcastle. Shearer is back on form!

- *25 June 1995*
  Alan Shearer agrees to extend his Blackburn Rovers contract for another three years...
- At the start of the 1995-96 season, Shearer's Blackburn record is 93 goals in 123 appearances.
- *30 December 1995*
  Scores against Chelsea – his goal makes history and Alan Shearer becomes the first player in football history to score 100 Premiership League goals. He is also the fastest ever Rovers player to notch up a goal score of 100.
- *17 April 1996*
  Shearer scores two goals to secure Blackburn's defeat of Wimbledon 3-2. His first goal (scored in the first 13 minutes of the match) makes history with Shearer becoming the first player since the 1930s to attain 30 goals in the top division in three consecutive seasons (1993-4: 31, 1994-5: 34, 1995-6: 31). The last 30-goaler was Jimmy Dunne for Sheffield United.
- *6 August 1996*
  Shearer returns to his birthplace – to 20,000 cheering fans in St James' Park.
- *14 September 1996*
  Newcastle beat Blackburn 2-1. Shearer scores against his old club.
- *28 December 1996*
  Scores two of the goals in the Newcastle v Spurs match that saw a 7–1 victory.
- *8 January 1997*
  Shearer's teacher, idol and friend, Kevin Keegan, resigns as manager of Newcastle.
- *15 January 1997*
  Kenny Dalglish is named as Keegan's successor. The Shearer-Dalglish partnership that worked so well for Blackburn, seems set to do the same for Newcastle.
- *1996-97*
  Shearer scores 25 League goals throughout the season.

HAT-TRICKS

- *9 April 1988*
  Becomes the youngest ever player to score a First Division hat-trick – in the first 49 minutes of the game – in Southampton's 4-2 defeat of Arsenal. This breaks Jimmy Greaves's record which has stood for 31 years. Shearer is aged 17 years and 240 days.
- *November 1994*
  Shearer takes Blackburn to the top of the League with his hat-trick against QPR in a 4-0 win.
- *18 November 1995*
  Shearer scores yet another stupendous hat-trick helping Blackburn to an amazing victory over Nottingham Forest – the final score is 7-0.

- *16 March 1996*
  During injury time, Shearer completes his first hat-trick of the season, giving Blackburn a 3-2 win over Tottenham at the Spurs' home ground.
- *2 February 1997*
  Shearer scores yet another charismatic hat-trick in the last 14 minutes of a game v Leicester – giving Newcastle a 4–3 victory.

INTERNATIONAL STARDOM

- *19 February 1992*
  Shearer makes his England debut against France at Wembley. The French side includes the former Manchester United star Eric Cantona, but this does not stop Shearer scoring his first national team goal, making his mark in a game that will see a 2-0 victory for England.
- *6 December 1995*
  Shearer finally scores a long-awaited European goal, from a penalty at Ewood Park, helping Blackburn to beat Rosenborg 4-1. Consequently the Norwegians are eliminated from the contest.
- *11 December 1995*
  Chosen by Terry Venables to play for England in a friendly against Portugal the following day.

- *8 May 1996*
  Named by Venables to play for England in an upcoming friendly v Hungary.
- *8 June 1996*
  A Shearer goal gives England the lead in their opening match v Switzerland. (A disputed penalty allows the Swiss to equalise in the second half.)
- *18 June 1996*
  Guarantees England a place in the last eight in Euro 96 as he and Teddy Sheringham score 4 goals against Holland at Wembley.
- *Euro 96*
  Shearer is the highest scoring player in the tournament with five goals in normal time.
- *30 August 1996*
  Hoddle appoints Shearer England captain (Tony Adams injured out) for the World Cup qualifying campaign.
- *1 September 1996*
  Shearer captains England for the first time, against Moldova in a game that sees England the 3-0 victors.
- *30 April 1997*
  Shearer scores one of the goals to beat Georgia at Wembley.
- *31 May 1997*
  Shearer misses a penalty kick but recovers his usual form by scoring one of England's goals. This helps give a 2–0 victory over Poland.
- *7 June 1997*
  A late Shearer strike gives England a 1–0 win over France at Le Tournoi.

TRANSFERS

- *24 July 1992*
  Joins Blackburn Rovers (from Southampton) for £3.3 million.
- *1996*
  Manchester United make Blackburn several offers for Shearer. The final bid of £12 milion is rejected.
- *29 July 1996*
  Shearer signs to childhood hero Kevin Keegan's Newcastle for a world record £15 million.

ALAN'S HONOURS

- Chosen from approximately 50 players nominated as part of the Rothmans' *Team of the Season* in the Rothmans' Football Honours 1995-96. The players are chosen by representatives of the Football Writers' Association: to be eligible, they must have appeared in FA Carling Premiership matches during the season.
- Attains 1st place in the 1995-96 FA Carling Premiership table notching up 37 goals: 31 League; 5 Coca-Cola Cup; 1 other cups (0 FA Cup).
- Nominated for FIFA World Player of the Year 1996. Comes 3rd with 123 points (1st = Barcelona's Ronaldo, the Brazilian International striker who notches up 329 points; 2nd = Liberian International George Weah (AC Milan) with 140 points).
- 1994-95 Footballer of the Year.
- 1997 PFA Player of the Year (Newcastle United).

INJURIES

- *December 1992*
  Crucial ligament damage puts Shearer out of the game for eight months.
- *18 April 1996*
  Undergoes scheduled groin operation to get him fit in time for Euro 96. Consequently misses the final two games of the season.
- *24 October 1996*
  Undergoes another groin operation. Afterwards is sidelined for six to eight weeks, causing him to miss England's World Cup match in Georgia.

- *25 February 1997*
  Shearer out for a minimum six club matches due to his third groin operation.
- *26 July 1997*
  During a friendly match v Chelsea, Shearer suffers yet another agonising injury: fracturing two bones, rupturing ligaments and displacing a joint. He is declared out of action for at least six months.

GREATEST ACHIEVEMENTS
- 31 league appearances
- 25 league goals (3 penalties)
- 1 Coca-Cola Cup goal
- 1 FA Cup goal
- 5 Premier League hat-tricks in the 1995-96 season.
- Before even making his debut with Southampton, Shearer scores 48 goals for the youth team.
- Scores 23 goals in 118 games with The Saints.
- Throughout his time at Blackburn, Shearer scores a total of 130 goals in just 165 games.
- Scores a total of 28 goals during the 1996-97 season: League 25; FA Cup 1; Coca-Cola Cup 1; Other Cups 1.
- By the end of the 1996-97 season, Shearer's overall goal score for England is 16 from 35 full caps.

CLUB HISTORY
Southampton
- Ground: The Dell, Milton Road, Southampton SO15 2XH.
- Ground capacity: 15,000.
- Year formed: 1880.
- Previous name: Southampton St Mary's.
- Nickname: 'The Saints'.
- Greatest score: 18 September 1965, Southampton beat Wolverhampton Wanderers 9-3.
- During the 1957-58 season (Division Three), Southampton scored their record number of League goals – 112.
- The most capped player in Southampton's history is Peter Shilton with 49 caps (England).
- Record transfer fee received in the club's history was £3.3 million paid by Blackburn Rovers for Alan Shearer.

Blackburn Rovers
- Ground: Ewood Park, Blackburn BB2 4JF.
- Ground capacity: 31,367.
- Year formed: 1875.
- Previous names: none.
- Nickname: 'Rovers'.
- Greatest score: 6 November 1954, Blackburn Rovers beat Middlesbrough 13-0.
- During the 1954-55 season (Division Two) Blackburn Rovers scored their record number of League goals – 114.
- The most capped player in Blackburn Rovers' history is Bob Crompton with 41 caps (England).
- Record transfer fee received in the club's history was the £15 million paid by Newcastle United for Alan Shearer.

Newcastle United
- Ground: St James' Park, Newcastle-upon-Tyne, NE1 4ST.
- Ground capacity: 36,610.
- Year formed: 1881.
- Previous names: Stanley; Newcastle East End.
- Nickname: 'Magpies'.
- Greatest score: 5 October 1946, Newcastle United beat Newport Co 13-0.
- During the 1951-52 season (Division One), Newcastle scored their record number of League goals – 98.
- The most capped player in Newcastle's history is Alf McMichael with 40 caps (Northern Ireland).
- Record transfer fee paid in the club's history was the £15 million to buy Alan Shearer from Blackburn Rovers.

Introduction by Robert Jeffery.
Robert Jeffery worked on local newspapers before helping to launch *Sky Sports Magazine*. He is currently a reporter on *FourFourTwo*, Britain's best-selling football magazine. He supports Wimbledon and Slough Town.

Main text by David Harding.
David Harding has worked as a journalist for newspapers, television and magazines (including *Kick It City* and *The Chelsea Independent*). He is a lifelong Chelsea supporter and his proudest footballing moment came when he was selected for Southampton Schoolboys – he was dropped after just one game. His ambition is to see Everton relegated.

The Foundry would like to thank Helen Burke, Helen Courtney, Helen Johnson, Lucinda Hawksley, Lee Matthews, Morse Modaberi and Sonya Newland for all their work on this project.

Picture Credits
All pictures © copyright Empics Sports Photo Agency